Holy Family
Coloring Book

Jesus, Mary & Joseph in Art

Written and illustrated by Katherine Sotnik

HOLY IMITATION® series

IGNATIUS PRESS   SAN FRANCISCO

*To all families,
especially the following:*

Robert & Tena Crosby and family
Alex & Barbara Cruz and family
James & Rita Deady and family
Dennis & Rose DeGoede and family
Bob & Theresa DeGoede and family
Patrick & Kathleen Kennedy and family
Dave & Anne Knappert and family
Pedro & Maria Perez and family
John & Anne Milas and family
Bill & Monica Rodio and family
Jerry & Ann Sargent and family
Tom & Liz Swartz and family

The Litany of the Holy Family prayer was reviewed and approved for use in private devotion by Most Reverend Alex J. Brunett, D.D., Ph.D., Archbishop of Seattle.

The artist gratefully acknowledges the permission granted to use the line drawing on page HF53, based on the original painting "Our Lady and Jesus Writing Characters" (Icon 15), courtesy of the Ricci Institute for Chinese-Western Cultural History at the University of San Francisco Center for the Pacific Rim.

The linework was rendered with technical ink pens on vellum. Several illustrations were drawn using computer drawing software with a pen tablet.

Holy Family Coloring Book by Katherine Sotnik
Copyright © 2012 The Sotnik Family Trust
Holy Imitation ® is a trademark of The Sotnik Family Trust

All rights reserved. No part of this book may be reproduced or transmitted in any form or by any means, electronic or mechanical, including photocopying, recording, or by any information retrieval systems without permission in writing from the publisher.

Published in 2012 by Ignatius Press, San Francisco
ISBN 978-1-58617-589-4
Printed by Thompson-Shore, Dexter, MI, (USA), Job # 585LS137, October 2012 ∞

Lord, have mercy on us.
Lord, have mercy on us.

Christ, have mercy on us.
Christ, have mercy on us.

Lord, have mercy on us.
Lord, have mercy on us.

Christ, hear us.
Christ, graciously hear us.

God the Father of heaven,
have mercy on us.

God the Son, Redeemer of the world, have mercy on us.

The Holy Family by Franz Ittenbach

God the Holy Spirit,
have mercy on us.

Holy Trinity, one God, have mercy on us.

Holy Family by Claudio Coello

Holy Family of Jesus, Mary and Joseph,
pray for us.

Holy Family, formed by the divine mystery, pray for us.

Based on *Madonna of Loreto* by Raphael Sanzio da Urbino

Holy Family, model of the Holy Trinity, pray for us.

Holy Family, of the House of David, pray for us.

The Adoration of the Shepherds by Gerard van Honthorst

HF15

Holy Family, venerated by the Church, pray for us.

Holy Family, icon of the domestic church, pray for us.

Coptic icon of the flight into Egypt

Holy Family, blessing for the human family, pray for us.

Holy Family, example for all Christian families, pray for us.

Holy Family, first model of families,
pray for us.

Holy Family, the Christmas family,
pray for us.

The Holy Family with the Infant Saint John the Baptist by Francesco de Mura

HF21

Holy Family, welcoming your first-born, the Messiah, pray for us.

Holy Family, visited by shepherds, pray for us.

The Nativity by Pompeo Batoni

HF23

Holy Family, beginning your life in the poverty of Bethlehem, pray for us.

Holy Family, offering two turtledoves for sacrifice, pray for us.

Presentation at the Temple by Giotto di Bondone

Holy Family, filled with wonder at Simeon's prophecy, pray for us.

Holy Family, accepting the gifts of the Magi, pray for us.

Holy Family, guided by angels on the flight into Egypt, pray for us.

Holy Family, nurtured by Mary,
pray for us.

Rest on the Flight to Egypt by Luc-Olivier Merson

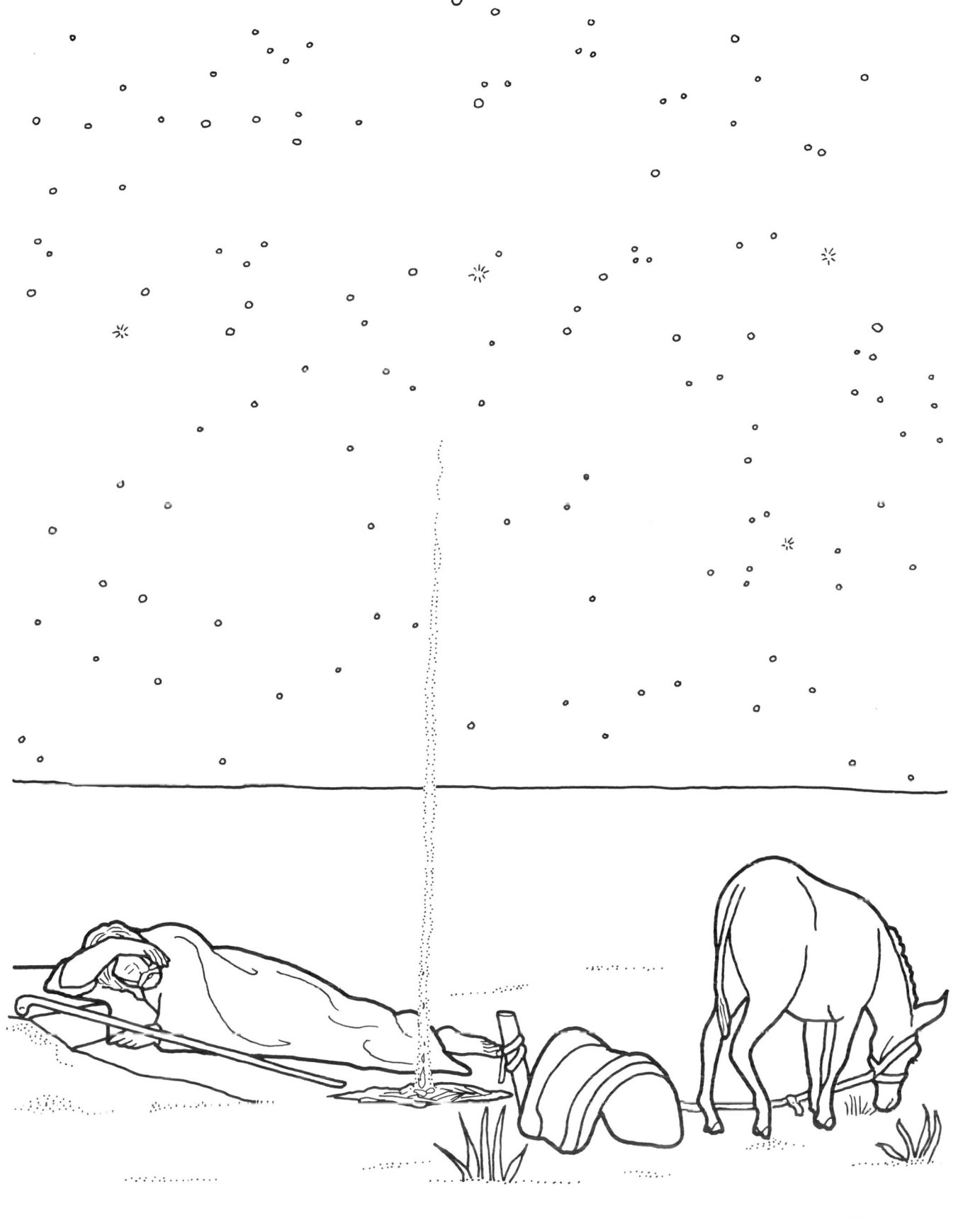

Holy Family, protected by Joseph, pray for us.

Holy Family, trusting in God,
pray for us.

The Holy Family by Raphael Sanzio da Urbino

Holy Family, sanctified by the presence of the Holy Child, pray for us.

Holy Family, living a hidden life in the House of Nazareth, pray for us.

Family of Nazareth, awaiting the fulfillment of God's promise, pray for us.

Holy Family by Ambrogio Lorenzetti

HF33

Family of Nazareth, suffering together after losing Jesus in the Temple, pray for us.

Jesus Lost by James Tissot

Jesus Found in the Temple by James Tissot

Family of Nazareth, rejoicing together after finding Jesus, pray for us.

Family of Nazareth, dignified by the hard work of the carpenter's shop, pray for us.

Jesus learning to help Joseph

Madonna of Loreto by Michelangelo Merisi da Caravaggio

Family of Nazareth, opening your home to neighbors and friends, pray for us.

Family of Nazareth, reflecting the sanctity of marriage, pray for us.

The Holy Family by Pompeo Batoni

Family of Nazareth, covenant of the fidelity of spouses, pray for us.

Family of Nazareth, consecrating the duty of fatherhood, pray for us.

Family of Nazareth, consecrating the mission of motherhood, pray for us.

Shrine of peace and love,
pray for us.

Shrine of purity and faith,
pray for us.

Shrine of kindness and truth,
pray for us.

Holy Family, centered on God,
pray for us.

Holy Family, a true human family,
pray for us.

Holy Family, open to life,
pray for us.

Holy Family, sanctuary of love,
pray for us.

Holy Family, cradle of life,
pray for us.

Holy Family, first educators in faith, pray for us.

The Holy Family by Benedetto Gennari II (the Younger)

Holy Family, school of patience and harmony, pray for us.

Holy Family, living image of God's love, pray for us.

Holy Family, suitable school
of education, pray for us.

Holy Family, rich in spiritual tenderness, pray for us.

Holy Family, witness to charity,
pray for us.

Holy Family, our hope in difficult trials, pray for us.

Holy Family, community of forgiveness, pray for us.

Holy Family, hope for each and every family, pray for us.

Holy Family, helping us to fulfill our daily tasks, pray for us.

Holy Family, teaching children to honor their parents, pray for us.

Holy Family, bringing broken families together again, pray for us.

Holy Family, calling families to conversion and prayer, pray for us.

Holy Family, spreading holiness over all the earth, pray for us.

Lamb of God, Who take away
the sins of the world,
spare us O Lord.

Lamb of God, Who take away the sins of the world, graciously hear us O Lord.

Lamb of God, Who take away
the sins of the world,
have mercy on us.

HF66 *The Holy Family by Franz Ittenbach*

Christ hear us.
Christ graciously hear us.

Let us pray.

O Lord God, allow the Holy Family to be present in a special way in our family and in all the families of the world.

Bless and protect our family,
nourish us with the sacraments...

The Rest on the Flight into Egypt by Francesco Vanni

The Flight Into Egypt by Gustave Doré

...and help us to "walk in today's world as a holy family".

We ask this through Christ our Lord.
Amen.